ESSAYS ON GOVERNMENT

JIM LYNCH

outskirts
press

To my dear wife Peggie,
Always at my side through
All of life's adventures

To my children,
Kathleen, Jim, and John—
May they continue to flourish

To my grandchildren,
Lucy, Vivianne, and Kara,
Jake and Eli,
Emmet and Nora—
May they learn from our mistakes

TABLE OF CONTENTS

Introduction

I write this small book primarily for my grandchildren. I am sure that at some future family gathering, perhaps 20 or 30 years from now, the question will be asked, why did he do it? Why at his age did he cash in all of his retirement savings and decide to become involved in presidential politics? What was he possibly thinking that made him believe that it would work? What was he trying to achieve?

I thought it would be helpful for those descendants of mine to have some firsthand information for the discussion. What their future judgment of me is not my great concern. I presume that twenty years from now I shall have ceased participating in discussions, political or otherwise. This book sets forth my objectives and political ideas in the winter of 2015. Hopefully, it will provide them with a window into my thoughts at the time.

What was I trying to achieve? I was 75 years old at the time. I had completed a long and successful career in administration for the Catholic Church. By all accounts, I should have been settling into a comfortable retirement of golf and travel. Instead, I became involved in the 2016 presidential primary. And I got involved in a big way. I became a candidate in the Iowa caucuses and the Missouri Republican presidential primary. And if the nomination had not been settled so abruptly on March 15, I intended to also participate in the Nebraska and South Dakota primaries.

My goal was modest. The objective was to get to the GOP National Convention in Cleveland in the summer of 2016 with a handful of delegates. I hoped to obtain somewhere between 100 and 200 delegates. If I could do that, I then wanted to present my ideas before the National Convention for discussion.

Some ideas were old ones that had been forgotten, and some were new and had never been discussed or tried. And I thought that if the convention became hopelessly deadlocked, maybe lightning might strike. Since I was only running for one term I might be chosen as a compromise nominee. Deadlocked political conventions in the past have produced unexpected results. Stranger things have happened. And you never know unless you get into the game.

My old ideas included balanced budgets and campaign finance reform. The new ideas proposed ways of curbing and reducing the national debt. I also laid out a plan for creating a manageable immigration policy and showed a way to provide for an affordable college education. My final new idea was a proposal for a universal commitment to national service.

In the summer of 2015, there were seventeen declared

Republican candidates for the Iowa caucuses. I could not see any of these individuals obtaining the necessary delegates to secure the nomination before the Cleveland Convention. I believed that the nominee would be chosen at the convention.

Besides presenting ideas for discussion, something else compelled me to get involved. It stirred in me a visceral reaction.

I saw evil coming down the road. It had visited America before. One form this evil took was of greedy Wall Street investment bankers. These were the sharp guys with their exotic financial investments that had caused the 2008 financial meltdown. They were contributing huge sums of money into the political campaigns. They hoped that this would insulate themselves from the reforms enacted after the Great Recession of 2008. It needed to be stopped. We did not want a repeat of the 2008 financial meltdown for which they were largely responsible.

I also saw the huge oil conglomerates trying to buy influence with their own large campaign donations. They wanted to keep their hold on world oil supplies. In the process, they had developed the bad habit of using the U.S. military to protect their interests. I believed that they had played a large part in the American invasion of Iraq. The Iraqi war cost the government in lives and in money. They needed to be held in check.

And also, I was alarmed by the actions of the large military industrial contractors. They were also making big contributions to some of the candidates. Armament firms thrive on war. It appeared that they were gearing up for another bite of the governmental apple. They wanted more military contracts. If they succeeded, they were likely to get us into more wars.

All these groups were thinking of themselves and not the good of the country. They needed to be stopped. But none of the announced candidates looked like they were even going to try to stop them. These were the reasons I decided to enter the fray.

I thought that I had one strong factor going for me. I believed the presidential election of 2016 was going to be the year of the outsider. Ordinary citizens had lost their trust in Washington. Yearly federal budgets were not being passed. Our foreign policy, especially in the Middle East, lacked clarity. The economy was still limping along, not fully recovered from the 2008 recession. And all the Democrats and Republicans in Congress seemed to do was bicker and blame each other for the current state of affairs. The average citizen was disgusted with Washington. So, if this was to be the year of the outsider, there was no one more an outsider to Washington than me.

I believed that good ideas were more important than money, and if properly presented would attract enough resources to finance a proper campaign. So, with the best of intentions, and after a long and distinguished career in administration, armed with my political science degree from Notre Dame and what money I could gather, I set off on this journey.

I hope that you find this small book interesting. I leave it to your good judgment whether you believe that it has any merit.

If anyone wishes to use any of the ideas in this book, please feel free to do so. I believe that America would be better by their implementation. I have kept this book as brief as possible. I see no need to try to write the complete history of the era. I am not a historian. This is just my story.

Chapter One

<hr>

THE SITUATION IN 2015

IT WAS A joyless time in America. The music reflected the mood. Melody and harmony had gone on holiday. They were replaced by loud noise with rude and rebellious lyrics.

The truth was under attack. It was being replaced by politeness. People were reluctant to speak freely on issues. All speech had to be politically correct. No one should say anything that might offend or make another person feel uncomfortable. The result was that people didn't say very much of substance. Truth died a slow death. Truth by its very nature is confrontational. The truth will always rail against falsehood.

Many people were confused and beginning to despair of ever achieving the American Dream. The middle class was shrinking. And those who had attained the American dream were not satisfied. They had achieved comfort but had not found happiness.

It did not seem that the country would ever recover from the financial collapse of 2008. Recent college graduates with staggering amounts of educational debt had few job prospects. Many were forced to move back home with their parents. And those who were employed saw their jobs outsourced overseas, or else made obsolete by robots. Workers were required to constantly improve their skills in order to just keep their jobs. The pace was hectic. Technology seemed to change every week. With the introduction of the internet, citizens were overwhelmed with more news and information than they could possibly absorb. People kept asking, where is all this leading?

In our cities, the police were facing an upsurge in gang violence. An opioid crisis affecting our young seemed to be sweeping the country.

Washington D.C. did not escape the chaos. Our foreign policy seemed to lack coherence. As a country, we were still trying to extricate ourselves from the Mideast quagmire of wars in Iraq and Afghanistan. But we seemed to be getting ourselves further involved in Syria. ISIS, an Islamic fundamentalist group, was attempting to form a new caliphate in a large area of Syria and in the northern part of Iraq. They seemed to be succeeding by the use of extreme ruthless measures. ISIS had to be stopped. The U.S. couldn't decide how to do it.

The political campaigns of the time were mean-spirited and

devoid of any mutual respect. They were designed to appeal to our deepest fears, rather than to our highest hopes. The political parties were at each other's throats. Discourse had given way to shouting, and compromise had descended into name calling. Annual budgets had not been passed in years.

The Affordable Care Act, which had been passed under the Obama administration, granted access to health care for millions of previously uninsured Americans. This was a good thing. However, adequate funding had not been provided. This together with a hemorrhaging Social Security system added to a spiraling federal budget deficit that was fast approaching twenty trillion dollars.

Despite having an elected Negro president, blacks were rioting in the streets of suburban St. Louis and in Baltimore. They were claiming police brutality and racial discrimination.

On top of all this, you had gay and lesbian groups marching in protest. They wanted their civil unions to have the same legal effect as a marriage. And they wanted the government to sanction any individuals or companies who did not honor their new status. This inflamed religious fundamentalists and others who thought that marriage was a union between a man and a woman.

Also, we had some individuals who wanted to change their gender. They marched for transgender rights, and the right to use whichever bathroom that they thought appropriate on any given day.

For the average citizen, events were moving too fast and seemingly without any rhyme or reason.

Americans blamed their elected officials for much of the situation. Budgets were not passed. The legislation was not enacted. The country was hurting. And the government seemed unable to act. Americans were mad. Or as one Iowa newspaper wrote, "they were mad as hell."

In the presidential politics of early 2015, two scenarios were coming into view. In the Democratic Party, it appeared that Hillary Clinton was going to be their presidential nominee. She had name recognition, experience, and a large campaign war chest. Her agenda harkened back to the mid-1990s when her husband Bill was president. Her campaign focused on progressive social policies, a sound fiscal policy, and an active global foreign policy.

Hillary's main Democratic challenger was Bernie Sanders, an independent Vermont senator who had recently become a Democrat. He espoused a modern form of socialism. He advocated Medicare coverage for all. This appealed to those who had no or very little health insurance. And he proposed that a college education should be free. This was especially appealing to college students and their parents. These and many other entitlements were all to be paid by increasing taxes on the rich. I was proved right in thinking that Bernie did not have much chance of winning. Hillary got the Democratic nomination.

On the GOP side in the summer of 2015, Jeb Bush was the clear leader. He had a record of accomplishment when he was governor of Florida. His campaign was well financed. And he had the Bush name. Both his father, George H. Bush, and his older brother, George W. Bush, had been president. He was being challenged by sixteen other candidates for the nomination. Some of these candidates seemed rather formidable. Below is a brief list of some of the other major candidates.

Dr. Ben Carson was a retired neurosurgeon and social conservative. His quiet intellectualism appealed to many, especially younger voters.

Chris Christie was the governor of New Jersey. He was a former federal prosecutor and was the current governor of New Jersey. He was plain speaking and aggressive. His pro-business policies in New Jersey appealed to many in the business community.

Ted Cruz was the senator from Texas. He had a strong following among Christian evangelicals and fiscal conservatives.

Marco Rubio was a senator from Florida. He was a young up-and-coming member of the GOP. He appealed to young voters.

The former Pennsylvania Senator Rick Santorem and Arkansas Governor Mike Huckebee, were both social conservatives.

George Pataki was the former governor of New York. He was a moderate Republican.

John Kasich was the current governor of Ohio. His strength was finance. He campaigned for a balanced budget.

There were also numerous business people running. The most notable of these was Donald Trump. He had made his fortune in real estate development. In the summer of 2015, he was considered more of a joke than a serious candidate.

And then there was Governor Scott Walker of Wisconsin. He had gained notoriety by challenging the powerful labor unions in his state.

With a large number of candidates, it looked like it could be a long and protracted nomination process. I believed the nomination would not be decided before the convention in Cleveland.

Hovering over all these candidates were the two main political parties. Traditionally, the political parties had been the steady anchors of American democracy. But now these political ships seemed to become loose from their moorings.

Democrats had always been the party of the working class. They were the party of the little guy. Democrats defended the rights of individuals against large corporations. It had been the party fighting for equality, jobs, and government assistance. Wealth was to be shared. The federal government should improve the lives of the poor and protect the unfortunate. Corporate greed should be held in check.

But now their focus seemed to shift. The Democratic Party adopted a strategy of identity politics. It decided to represent groups instead of individuals. The party became obsessed with defending minority rights: women's rights, gay rights, black lives matter, transgender bathrooms, etc. They were strongly pro-choice and supported government subsidized abortions. Many of their working middle class supporters seemed to be baffled by all this.

The Republican Party had changed in a different manner. The GOP had always been the party of individual freedom, of unlimited opportunity, of small government and fiscal restraint. They thought that individual initiative should be encouraged and unrestrained. No limits should be placed on accomplishments or wealth. But now the party seemed to be splintered by a number of single-issue groups.

One was a group composed of evangelical Christians. This group was pro-life and against abortion, against same-sex marriage, and against a federally mandated school curriculum. They were strong supporters of Israel. They practiced a literal interpretation of the Bible, and were against the teaching of evolution in public schools. They hoped to create a new civil society in preparation for the end of the world and the second coming of Christ.

Another group of Republicans was obsessed with the notion that President Obama was going to appear at their front door and take away their guns. They were adamant about preserving their second amendment right to have guns. This concern was fueled by the National Rifle Association. The NRA, as they were called, fanned this paranoia and supplied large quantities of cash to candidates who supported their position.

Still another group was obsessed by the number of illegal

immigrants entering the country from Mexico and Central America. They wanted a wall built across our southern border to keep these immigrants out of the country.

Big business wanted fewer government regulations and lower corporate taxes.

The super-wealthy, or 1% as they were called, wanted lower taxes.

All of this greatly troubled me. The country was facing some severe problems, but none of the candidates were addressing those issues, nor seemed capable of rectifying the situation. It appeared to me that some of the candidates were in the presidential primaries for personal glory, some for the money, and some candidates were just acting as substitutes for special interest groups. The question that I was faced with was, with all that was going on, did I just sit and watch, or should I become involved? I decided to act.

You must remember that I had come of age during the time of President Kennedy. I was an avid supporter of his. His speeches were beautifully crafted and uplifting. He and his family seemed perfect. They projected a sense of charm and elegance. He made me proud and happy to be an American. In his inauguration speech, he said, "Ask not what your country can do for you, but ask what you can do for your country." It was a magical time. I was all in. After college graduation, I returned to Chicago and volunteered at the local Democratic organization.

But things changed. Kennedy was assassinated. Next Martin

Luther King and Bobby Kennedy were killed. Lyndon Johnson became president. The country became involved in the Vietnam War and could not find a way out of it.

I married Peg, and we started a family and moved to the suburbs. Eventually, I was hired by the Catholic Diocese of Joliet. It was comprised of most of the suburban counties that surrounded Chicago. I was the Director of Administration, which meant that I oversaw the business and financial aspects of the diocese. It was a big job. I enjoyed it and the people with whom I worked. We built a lot of new churches. We helped a lot of people. We did a lot of good. I worked there for twenty-seven years until I retired.

In college, I had studied government and politics. I had a political science degree from the University of Notre Dame. Through the years I had kept up an interest in politics. However, having a visible position working for the Church, I did not think it appropriate to be involved in partisan politics.

When I decided to become involved in politics again, my first decision was which party would I join? As I said previously, I had started my adult life as a Democrat. But by 2015 I was a registered Republican. Sometime in the 1980s I had registered as a Republican. And for the life of me, I can't remember why I did it. I presume that there was a contested primary race which generated my interest. In Illinois, in order to vote in a primary contest, you have to declare for a party. In truth, by 2015 I was more of an independent. And I was looking for a political party. I must admit that I was conflicted about this. By temperament and emotion, I was a Democrat. I wanted to help people. But by logic and reason, I felt like a Republican. What you can accomplish is limited by your resources.

I eventually decided to participate in the Republican primary process. Neither party was perfect. I was pro-life, and I wanted a sound fiscal policy. These issues were part of the Republican platform. I guess I just felt more comfortable with the Republicans.

Chapter Two

THE MAIN PROBLEM

AMERICA WAS GOING broke. This was the number-one problem facing the country. We were on an unsustainable path of spending more money than our tax revenue was generating. This conduct was currently sustained by increased borrowing. But just as individuals cannot borrow their way to wealth, neither can a nation sustain itself by borrowing.

History has shown what happened to other great nations that followed this path.

Spain was a powerful European country that once ruled a large portion of the Western Hemisphere. This lasted as long as the Spanish Crown had the mineral wealth of the New World to shore up its treasury. But once that source dried up, its status as a world power declined.

The British Empire suffered the same fate. It was said that the sun never set on the English flag. Through their trade and naval strength, England became a great world power. But after World War Two, their finances contracted, and they were no longer a world power. If America does not want to follow the path of Spain and England, then it has to get its financial house in order.

We needed a balanced budget, and not only a balanced budget, but we needed a budget with a surplus. We needed a surplus so that we could begin to reduce our national debt, which was approaching twenty trillion. And we needed to do this now.

The way to balance the federal budget was to increase revenue either by expanding the economy, which would generate more tax revenue, or by increasing corporate and personal taxes. It is also necessary to reduce all nonessential spending.

I proposed a way to reduce the debt. It was a national debt reduction program. This program would be similar to what the average citizen experiences in paying their home mortgage. We should amortize the national debt just like a home mortgage. If it takes twenty or twenty-five years to pay off the national debt, so be it. But we must start paying down the national debt now!

The experts in Congress say that we can have a balanced budget in ten years. That is nonsense! Why not a balanced budget this year, or next year at the latest? Will this be difficult? You bet it will be. But if we do nothing, how can we ever hope to face our grandchildren? Are we going to leave them to pay for our irresponsible behavior?

How we got into this predicament is a matter of dispute. The Republicans blame the Democrats, and the Democrats blame the Republicans. I believe there were several factors that contributed to the huge deficit. The first factor began unwittingly and unnoticed in the 1990s. It was during the heady years of the Clinton administration. At that time America had a surplus in its treasury.

Congress let the genie out of the bottle when the Glass-Steagall Act was repealed. That act, which Congress passed in 1933, restricted banks from using their customers' money to invest in the stock market. Its purpose was to prevent banks from speculating in stocks. This conduct during a down stock market could potentially weaken a bank's capital. Stocks were considered capital on a bank's balance sheet. Banks can only lend a certain percentage of their capital. A decrease of capital could force a bank to cease lending, and in some cases to call in some of their existing loans. This happened during the 1929 crash. It almost happened to some of the nation's large banks in the recession of 2008. Without the assistance of the federal government, which purchased many of their loans, many of the large banks would have become insolvent. This required action by the federal government increased the national debt by trillions. At the time the Glass-Steagall Act was repealed; most people never imagined the wild chaos that it would later fuel. While the act's repeal was in the 1990s, its real impact was not felt until the 2008 recession.

The next step occurred in the administration of George W. Bush. When he assumed the presidency there was still a surplus in the Treasury. His cavalier policies, however, eroded this surplus. First, he expanded the Medicare prescription drug program. This decision increased his popularity with voters. But there was not sufficient additional funding provided for it. This produced a big hit to the surplus fund. Next, he led the U.S. into under funded wars in Afghanistan and Iraq. And suddenly the surplus was gone.

In 2008, we had the great recession. Greedy Wall Street traders played a major part in it. They had developed and then sold an assortment of exotic mortgage securities. These securities were traded by many of the banks that had been released from restraints on such trades by the Glass-Steagall Act repeal. Many of these instruments proved to be either worthless or of little value. When the value of these securities dropped, the balance sheets of many banks froze.

To save the banks from insolvency, it was necessary for the federal government to purchase these securities of dubious value. If the large financial institutions could not open for business, our whole financial system would have come crashing down. This dire financial scenario was averted. But the price we paid to do this was to greatly increase our national debt.

And finally, President Obama added to the national debt when he persuaded the Congress to pass the Affordable Care Act. This was a well-intended piece of legislation that provided health insurance for many people who had been unable to purchase it in the past. But despite the good intentions, the act was underfunded by trillions of dollars. Add this all up and you have a national debt that is approaching 20 trillion. And it keeps rising as we continue to have deficit budgets.

America has borrowed all this money which will someday have to be repaid. Right now, America is a debtor nation. Investors from around the world are still willing to lend money for us to operate. But at some point, they will ask for their money back.

The sharp guys on Wall Street tell us not to worry. They say we can always just print more money. This, of course, will devalue all of our assets. Or if that does not work, they say inflation will take us out of this problem. The idea is that we would pay off our debt with cheaper dollars than what we borrowed. Now wouldn't that be slick? But does America want to be slick? Or does it want to be honorable? We must remember that these are the sharp guys with their convoluted mortgage documents who brought us the 2008 recession.

Not only did we have a federal financial problem, but we also had many state financial problems. The Affordable Care Act said that part of the funding for the new health coverage was to come from the state governments. But more sick people than expected joined the insurance plans. Some of the states had not budgeted for the higher numbers. Other states just didn't have the money to pay their share of the insurance cost. Many states were already scrambling to pay their own underfunded pension liabilities. Obamacare has driven most of the states deeper into debt.

All of these problems were coming at a time when we needed to improve our military hardware and to improve our crumbling infrastructure.

So, what do we do to solve these problems? There are two ways to balance the federal budget. One deals with increasing federal revenue, the other with reducing federal spending.

First, let's deal with increasing the revenue. The economy has to be energized. This will increase business tax revenue. Part of the way to do this would be by revising the federal tax code. And not only revising it but greatly simplifying it. For a tax code to be respected and obeyed it must be seen as fair. Our present code has through the years been subjected to constant rule changes. Every lobbyist and interest group has been at work to get special rules enacted for their group. As a result, the current code is bewildering to the professionals and totally incomprehensible to the general public. And it was certainly seen as unfair by the average citizen.

For the individual tax system to be fair, it will mean that everyone pays some tax. In 2015 43% of Americans paid no federal income tax. This has to end until we have paid off the national debt. If you are super-wealthy and have a large number of write-offs, you should still have to pay some tax. And if you are at the bottom end of the economic spectrum, you should also pay a federal tax. It may only be $5.00 per month, but you should still be required to contribute to reducing the federal deficit. We are all in this situation together. We are all Americans. No one gets a free ride.

Whatever the new tax bill will be, it should increase the nation's revenue. With our country's current financial condition, it would make no sense to decrease tax revenue. And as a definite exclamation point, I did not believe that the federal estate tax should be eliminated. We need all the revenue that can be generated.

Corporate taxes also should be modified. The current corporate rate of 35% should be reduced. 20% might be a logical target. But to compensate for a rate deduction, we must end the practice of American companies keeping their funds in offshore banks that are not subject to U.S. taxes. We should have a moratorium period where these offshore funds can be returned to the U.S. with only a moderate tax on them. After that, if any U.S. company wants to continue keeping its capital outside of the U.S., it will be required to pay a 15% tariff on all goods sold in the U.S. That includes on goods made outside or inside the country. America is the world's largest consumer market. If you are going to use our market, then it is only fair that your company contribute to the country. If you are going to play, then you are going to pay! The practice of companies setting up foreign domiciles to avoid paying taxes must be stopped. Needless to say, changes to our corporate tax code must increase the nation's tax revenue.

To do this right will be the most difficult. A lot of enemies will be created along the way. That is why I thought my candidacy had a distinctive advantage. I was only running for one term. In pushing through this and other tough legislation, the president cannot be thinking about reelection. His emphasis must be on doing what he believes to be right, and what will improve the good of the country. This concludes my thoughts on increasing revenue.

Let's now turn to the spending items which must be curtailed.

First on this list must be reducing the government's health-care costs. This is one issue in which I claimed to have some expertise. While working for the Church I was involved in establishing numerous insurance pools— property, casualty, and health. I had an understanding of what the Affordable Care Act was trying to achieve.

Reducing the nation's health-care costs will not be easy. It is complicated because there are so many groups who must participate in the solution for it to be effective. The doctors, the drug companies, and the hospitals must all be on board. And there must be the will to take on the trial lawyers, and the pharmaceutical and insurance companies.

The doctors and the hospitals can be brought on board if there is meaningful tort reform. By tort reform, I mean legal limits must be placed on medical malpractice awards. This would free both the hospitals and doctors from having to pay exorbitant yearly liability insurance premiums. Currently, they pay these premiums to protect themselves from multimillion-dollar lawsuits. To achieve tort reform we have to take on the trial lawyers and their lobbyists (nothing worthwhile is ever easy). These measures would reduce the cost to both doctors and hospitals. It would follow that most of these savings would be passed on to consumers as lower medical costs. This would reduce the cost of Medicare and Medicaid.

Drug costs could be reduced by speeding FDA approval of new drugs, and allowing or threatening to allow greater access to foreign drugs.

I believed that it would be easier if the Affordable Care Act was reformed, rather than repealed. A careful reform could bring about the same result as a new health act. Reforming the Affordable Care Act could be done with much less time and effort than starting all over again.

The final piece of insurance reform would be to have a single health payer system instituted. This payer can be either the government or a single not-for-profit outside provider. This would reduce the cost of administering the government insurance programs. Programs that are administered by insurance companies always add their own overhead and profit to their administering costs. The single-payer system would eliminate the profit costs. This should reduce the overall cost of the insurance programs by 15 to 20%.

The central idea behind insurance is that of shared risk. The larger the insurance pool, then the lower the individual cost. If you have a small health insurance pool with only the sick participating, then all you are doing is paying claims, and the cost is going to be very high for the individual insured. In a true national health-care system, everyone must be insured. If they don't have private insurance, then they must be in the government program. No exceptions! Everyone participates in the Social Security program, and the world has not ended. The same can be said for insurance. For the pool to be successful, individual costs must be kept reasonable; the program must include the healthy as well as the sick.

Social Security is the next entitlement program to be addressed. This will not be as difficult as health care to resolve. But it must be done to stop the drain on the Treasury. All earned income must be subject to Social Security contribution. This will affect the higher-income brackets. And for everyone under the age of 50, it will require a slight increase in the contribution and by raising of the retirement age to age 67.

There are a few more issues that should be addressed in regards to the financial issues. Many of our state governments are under financial stress. Many state pension funds are grossly underfunded. The additional burden on states of increased Medicare funding has not been properly anticipated and funded. So while the federal government would like to push much of the health-care costs on to the states, in reality, this approach is not feasible. The states do not have the money to absorb these costs. Health insurance costs will be best served if they are addressed at the federal level.

All these financial issues are solvable. But the longer we delay in attacking them, the harder the solution becomes. It has been said that there is never a good time to do a difficult task, and there is never a bad time to postpone doing one. Now is the time to curb our national debt and to bring the country's finances under control. Each day the national debt increases. If not now, when do we correct the situation?

Chapter Three

CAMPAIGN FINANCE REFORM

WE ALMOST HAD it. In the run-up to the 2008 Presidential Election the candidates, John McCain, the Republican, and Barack Obama, the Democrat, initially agreed to limit their campaign spending to what the federal guidelines prescribed. That would have been an $84.1 million limit for each candidate.

Then Barack Obama met with the boys on Wall Street. They offered him wheelbarrows full of money. He decided to withdraw from the spending agreement. John McCain stayed true to his word. He limited his spending to the amounts in the federal guidelines. Obama won the election, and we heard no more about campaign finance reform. Practicality triumphed over principle. When this happens, it is never a victory for the country.

Currently, we have a very corrupt government in Washington. It is corrupt by the way it allows and even encourages money to influence it. I am not saying that all elected officials are bad. Nor am I saying anything derogatory about the many dedicated civil service employees. For the most part, I think they do an admirable job. What I am saying is that the current system of campaign financing is rotten and needs to be changed.

Part of the problem is with the elected officials. It shows itself when their desire to be reelected becomes more important than serving the people who elected them. There is no doubt that having more cash to spend in an election than your adversary is an advantage. Currently, it is estimated that a quarter to a half of each congressman's working hours are spent trying to raise funds for future elections. This diminishes the time they have for promoting or understanding legislation. This is not right.

But this is not the biggest campaign finance disgrace. In this sorry mess that honor goes to the professional lobbyists. They accept money from various individuals, corporations, foundations, committees, and also from foreign governments. The lobbyists' stated purpose is to either promote or defeat various legislative bills. They do this through the logic of their cause and through the persuasion of their political contributions— mostly by their contributions.

To see how this works all you have to do is follow the money. It was reported that in 2013 the government of China gave to lobbyists in Washington D.C. over $1.3 billion. Of this money, the lobbyists take their 10 or 15% off the top. They have expenses to cover. The remainder of the money is then spread around to those congressmen and senators who promote the Chinese agenda.

The elected officials then use this money in their reelection campaigns to purchase radio, television, and newspaper ads. So you have three different groups in this food chain.

Who is going to stop this? The lobbyists aren't. They are making good money from this. The congressmen and senators will not. They are getting money for their next campaigns. And the news media certainly won't. This is a steady revenue stream for them. It helps the profit. It protects their jobs. This is just an example of the workings of one foreign government. Imagine how many other countries and foreign and domestic companies participate in the process. Washington D.C. is awash in illegal money flowing towards our elected officials. This is wrong.

Money and wealthy people will always have a place in a democratic society. But society will only be well served when that money is used to debate the issues, and not to hinder the election process.

You would think that the Supreme Court would be a bulwark against this conduct. But the Court further complicated the campaign finance issue with their Citizens United decision. This decision had some far-reaching implications which I am not sure the Court anticipated. The decision said that corporations had the same free speech rights as ordinary citizens. And it followed from that logic that since corporations had the right to protected free speech, they also had the right to make political campaign contributions. This added more money to already overflowing political campaigns.

Since most corporations are very pro-business, this greatly helped the GOP. This was bad law. It further infused more money into the election process. Elections became spending contests. Further compounding the situation was that various committees and foundations could also contribute. This allowed the identification of the donors to be hidden.

I have just described the problem. Now how do we correct the situation? You probably have to solve it incrementally. The first step should be to overturn the Citizens United decision. This would curtail the large amounts of corporate money in the campaigns. This can be done if properly pursued through the courts. There must be limits on what a corporation can donate to a political campaign. Congress also needs to enact legislation on reasonable campaign spending limits. But will Congress pass any meaningful laws that will reduce the flow of money to it? I doubt it.

Hopefully, a cadre of disciplined and dedicated politicians will appear who will be willing to make the hard choices to bring about reform. We need to develop a common formula to curb what can be spent on a political campaign. This formula could be based on the population of each congressional district or the population of each state. If raising ever-increasing sums of money is removed from the concerns of our politicians, hopefully, they will use their newfound time to better concentrate on legislative issues. Their time can be better spent than on raising money.

This issue is critical to solving our nation's financial issues.

I'd be remiss if I did not mention another matter that the Supreme Court is crucial in solving. The court is the final arbitrator on individual freedom issues. Currently, individual freedom is being placed above that of the common good of all our citizens. If the court does not change its current direction on this issue, we will have a country where any conceivable individual right is guaranteed, but a country in which nothing functions! Individual rights cannot override the common good of society.

Chapter Four

FOREIGN POLICY

SIMPLY STATED, THE purpose of our foreign policy is to protect American interests and United States citizens both at home and abroad.

Our nation's foreign policy is governed by treaties with foreign governments, presidential acts and declarations, and congressional laws. To have a credible foreign policy, first and foremost we must keep our word to our treaty partners. Also, our policies must be clear to ourselves and to the rest of the world. And we must be consistent in our actions.

To defend our borders and our international interests, we must maintain a strong military. This necessitates a high level of defense spending. Our foreign policy also means protecting those American citizens abroad who are engaged in legitimate pursuits. It requires that we have skillful diplomats to advance America's economic, political, and peace interests among other governments around the world. Another essential ingredient of a good foreign policy is to be predictable. Our friends and foes should have a clear idea of our policies and how we will act in certain situations. What we will do if one of our allies is attacked should be crystal clear. What we will not tolerate in conduct from other countries should also be clear.

It is Congress's responsibility to fund America's foreign policy efforts. This requires bipartisanship support for all major foreign policy initiatives. We can't be changing our relationships with countries every time we change governments. Our allies must have confidence that we are going to honor our agreements. If we are going to be changing our commitments every four or eight years, no country will seriously want to enter into treaties with us.

Democracies by their nature are very difficult to manage. Nothing is more difficult to manage than a country's foreign policy. A democracy has many moving parts that have to be maneuvered in order to accomplish any good result.

I believe we complicate our foreign policy when we try to sell democracy to the rest of the world. Democracy may not work for every country. For democracy to succeed you need a solid judiciary, a stable government, and an educated electorate. Every country does not have all these components.

In America, democracy has worked. Because of our experience, we have developed the idea that it should work for every country. If they would adopt it, then they would be happy and prosperous. This is not always true. Greece is a modern-day example of this failure.

There are two ways of spreading democracy. One way is through aggressive salesmanship, which we have tried. The other is by a good example. I believe the United States would be better served if we spent our energy on making America a more exemplary democracy. If we can do that, I believe other nations would follow our example. Until then we should support those governments, whatever their form, which allow and encourage their citizens to develop to their full capabilities.

America is currently at a crossroads. We need to refine our idea of who we are as a nation and how we want to present ourselves to the rest of the world. What does America stand for? What are the American ideals? Traditionally, America has stood for freedom, for equality, for an opportunity, and for justice. If these are our ideals, then we must try to live up to them.

To an outsider, it seems that the U.S.'s only goal is to sell economic prosperity and technology to the rest of the world. Perhaps we should add the civic virtues of honesty, decency, fairness, loyalty, and strength of purpose to our sales brochure and to our conduct.

In addition to being strong militarily, we need to be strong economically. A debtor nation cannot lead with authority forever. If we do not sustain our economic power, we will go the way of former world powers. Spain, France, and Great Britain.

We were involved in two armed conflicts in the Middle East—neither one of which we should have been in. We had been in Afghanistan for almost 15 years. Our original purpose in going into Afghanistan was to silence Osama bin Laden and his followers. He and his followers were responsible for the September 11, 2001 attacks. We initially achieved that objective. But then through our American hubris, we decided to create a democratic society in Afghanistan. In essence, we tried to impose a Western-style democratic government on a tribal society. So far this has failed.

We invaded Iraq to rid it of weapons of mass destruction. We found none. But that did not stop us from trying to establish a democratic form of government there as well. This also failed. Iraqi society had existed for many centuries. But we thought that we would install our legal system. They had their own legal system that dated back to the time of Hammurabi. It was in place for almost three thousand years. From the start, our approach in Iraq was doomed to failure. We tried to install a two-hundred-year-old American democracy on a four-thousand-year-old culture. Time has proven the folly of our deeds. National hubris has consequences which are measured in lives and resources lost.

The reasons for our invasion of Iraq have always been dubious. Ostensibly, it was to rid the country of the weapons of mass destruction possessed by Saddam Hussein and his partisans. These were never found. We had no plan for controlling the country after the invasion. We had no coordinated policy for administering the various ethnic groups. The result was we decided to support the Shiite faction of the population against the Sunni faction. The Shiite faction was quickly taken over by their Iranian cousins. The effect of our blunders has been disastrous for the people of Iraq and their country. When the invasion began, there were 500,000 Christians living peacefully in Iraq. Currently, there are reported to be only 25,000 remaining. Most of the Christians were either killed or put to flight.

We lost in Iraq. More than all the dire statistics, more than the loss of young American lives, and more than the great cost in Iraqi lives and property was the loss of a very bedrock American foreign policy principle. We had never attacked another country without provocation. In the Iraqi war, there was no provocation towards us. We were the aggressor.

How do we remedy this situation? I proposed that we should withdraw from both countries in the quickest and most honorable way possible. We needed to come to the realization that we cannot fix all the problems in the world. And that the American style of democratic government is not necessarily applicable throughout the whole world.

Chapter Five

IMMIGRATION

UNLIKE THE WARS in Iraq and Afghanistan, the issue of immigration does not require detachment. It requires more engagement on our part. Currently, we have refugees coming to America in record numbers. They come from the Middle East, from Africa, and from Asian nations. We also have people from Mexico, Central America, and the Caribbean coming to America. Everyone comes in search of jobs and a better life. We are being overwhelmed by immigrants. We have an immigration system that has not been updated since 1965.

Until 1965 America's primary immigration came in waves from different European countries. They spoke different languages and had different religions. But they all had the same cultural outlook on life. Their outlook was based on a long Judeo-Christian tradition. This tradition was based on the Ten

Commandments and amplified by the Christian Beatitudes. This outlook was administered through the courts by the English common law. This amalgamation of people and tradition seemed to work. America prospered and became a vibrant society.

In 1965 we revised our immigration laws to allow many more people from Asia, Africa, and the Middle East to come to America. They also came seeking a better life. They all wanted the American dream. But their backgrounds, for the most part, were very different from the previous immigrants. These new immigrants had different customs and beliefs. This was unsettling for some Americans, who saw this trend as an erosion of our culture.

At the same time, we had a huge influx of people crossing our border from the south. They were coming for economic reasons and for their personal safety. This influx was encouraged by a 1986 amnesty bill which gave temporary legal status to illegal aliens who were fleeing persecution in their own country. If you could make it to America and show that you were coming from a country where you might be persecuted, you could stay in America. Not only could you stay, but you could bring your family, either with you or after you entered the country. These immigrants were predominantly Spanish-speaking with no knowledge of the English language. They had no resources when they entered the country. They placed a great burden on the social, medical, and educational expenses of both the federal and state governments. But while they did not speak English, for the most part, they did share the Judeo-Christian outlook on life.

And to add to this influx, we had wealthy people from China coming to America to give birth to children who will automatically become American citizens. This way of acquiring citizenship should be stopped.

It is necessary to update our immigration laws. And we also must increase the security on our southern borders. One of the other candidates suggested that we build a wall across our southern border. This may slow the influx of migrants. But my guess is that if they can't come on land, then they will come by boat. The problem is systemic. Poor people seeking work.

This situation is similar to what America faced after World War Two. At that time Europe was devastated. There were few jobs. Everyone wanted to come to the United States where they could work. Congress solved the problem by creating what became known as the Marshall Plan. In essence, we said, Stay where you are. We shall loan you money to rebuild your countries. This will give you work, and allow you to stay in place. This is what is needed for Southern Mexico, Central America, and the Caribbean.

I called this idea the Caribbean Recovery Act. I was the only candidate to propose something like this. My proposal was similar but not the same as the original Marshall Plan. In the Caribbean Recovery Act monies would not have been given directly to the governments. The monies would have gone directly to the projects. The payments would be made directly to either local companies or to American companies who would have hired local tradesmen. The governments would have been given a small fee—perhaps 10% for the processing of permits for the projects. The monies for the projects would be considered loans to be repaid over time.

Currently, we are spending our money on welfare, educational, and policing costs associated with the illegal immigrants who enter this country. The U.S. should use these monies to improve the poor areas of the region. Over time this would be less expensive for us.

And most migrants would sooner work in their native country. Very few people want to leave home. They do not want to leave their family and friends.

Maybe in the future, some politician will pick up the torch and bring this idea back to the public forum for consideration.

In order to solve our immigration problems, I thought we should focus on one problem at a time. I proposed that we place a moratorium on immigration from the Middle East, the African continent, and from Asia. We should concentrate our time and resources on trying to solve the influx of people from this hemisphere. Once that problem is solved, then we could turn our attention to immigrants from other parts of the world.

There's no doubt we have to improve our border security. This can be accomplished by increased border patrols, electronic surveillance systems, or some permanent walls. But this will only slow the inflow. It will not stop it.

There's been a great deal of talk about building a wall across the southern border. Our border is over two thousand miles long.

That is the distance from Chicago to Los Angeles. I don't think that a wall that long will ever be built. But even if it could be built, it's not going to solve the problem.

Instead of coming by land the immigrants will come by water. So instead of coming through El Centro, California, El Paso or Laredo, Texas, they'll be coming by boat into San Diego, La Jolla, Galveston, and New Orleans. These are desperate people. They are being driven by poverty and fear. They can't earn a living in their hometown, so they hop a freight train, ride buses, or walk across hot deserts, just for the opportunity of cutting grass, washing dishes, and picking our fruits and vegetables.

In conclusion, we should focus on solving one immigration problem at a time. And we should try to solve the immigration problems at their source, and not wait until the problem is at our border.

Chapter Six

———— ∾ ————

DEFENSE AND EDUCATION

IN ORDER TO successfully execute our foreign policy, it's necessary to have a strong military force.

What our military needed more than ever was some rest. We had been at war since 2002. It started in Afghanistan and then spread to Iraq. Our service personnel and our military equipment were worn out. It was time to bring our armies home. It was time to modernize our military equipment.

Not only were the soldiers tired, but morale was low. There are two things that we could do to improve morale. First, we could increase the pay of our military servicemen and -women. They were underpaid for what we asked them to do. And second, we could improve the veterans' medical facilities. In most cases the waiting time for our vets to receive medical attention was outrageous. Some veterans were dying before they were able to see a doctor.

It would be necessary to increase spending on military hardware. All branches of the service needed to have modernized new equipment.

While we increased our military funding, we also needed to tighten up our procurement procedures. It boggled my mind when I heard the amount of the cost overruns on some of our military contracts. A bid should mean something. If a contractor can't bring the product in at the contract price, then the contractor should eat the difference. The government should not bear the contractor's mistakes. Open competitive bidding on many nonsensitive defense projects would do a lot to reduce the cost of updating our military.

We should also increase the size of our military. And this leads me into my next very controversial idea.

I proposed that all able-bodied individuals between the ages of seventeen and twenty-seven be required to give a minimum of two years' service to the country. This would consist of six weeks of basic military training, and then the balance would be spent on various activities of the inductees' choice. It could be spent in the military. Or it might be in the Environmental and Conservation Corp. There they would focus on improving the environment, such as cleaning streams, lakes, and rivers. Or the inductee's service could be with the Build America Corporation. There they would be involved in restoring our housing stock, improving our sidewalks, and other aspects of our infrastructure. Or they could be involved in teaching in impoverished areas in Appalachia or along our southern border.

For this service, each participant would receive an educational voucher for two years of tuition, room, and board at any state college in their home state that they qualified to attend. If they choose to spend four years in service, then they will get a voucher for four years of college. The result would be that a child of a poor or middle-income family, who enters the program at 18, could have a college degree and be debt free by age twenty-six. They could then get on with their life. They would be free to marry, buy a house, or live independently without the burden of educational debt hanging over them.

This would be much better than giving students free education, as is often talked about. The young people would have earned their education. They would have the pride of accomplishment. And the nation would have received the benefit of their services. Also, the young people would have contributed to their country. They would have skin in the game, so to speak.

There would be other benefits from this program.

This mandatory service would decrease the pool of young men who could be recruited into the inner-city gangs. There would be fewer idle young people in the neighborhoods. And the young men and young women who had never been outside of their neighborhood would get a chance to see other parts of the country. They would see what a big world there is out there.

America was becoming an economically fragmented society.

People with wealth tend to live in protected and gated compounds. This allows bigotry and misinformation to thrive. This program would defuse some of the misinformation about certain segments of our society. Poor kids would see that all rich kids were not insensitive and callous. And the wealthier kids would see the poorer kids as individuals, reducing their fear of them. World War Two did a great job of homogenizing American society. Service to the country would take some much-needed steps in that direction.

National service will not clean up all of our rivers and streams. It will not rebuild all of our blighted communities. And it will not eliminate the inner-city gang problems. But it will go a long way towards reducing them. I hope someday mandatory service to the country will be tried.

Chapter Seven

FAMILIES

FAMILIES ARE THE cornerstone of any community. They were the foundation on which American society grew and developed. They were part of the American Dream. The Dream was to be able to properly shelter, feed, clothe, and educate a family. Until recently we were a country of families.

But over the last fifty years or so people have become more mobile. First, it was a move to suburbia. Then it was a job transfer to another city. Children started going to school out of state. And they did not return. The old neighborhoods changed. New people moved in. Family members no longer lived close to each other. This accelerated the process of going from a nation of families to a nation of individuals. We have to go back to being a nation of families. And we have to do all we can to strengthen the family unit. And I mean from start to finish.

This leads us into a discussion of a very volatile issue: abortion. How do we protect the unborn? When does a fetus become a person? And what rights does a woman have over her own body? These are all explosive issues. On one side you have the pro-life group that says that life begins at conception, and must be protected from conception to birth. On the other side, you have pro-choice groups that hold that a woman has the right to control her own body and to terminate a pregnancy at any time prior to birth.

These are heated issues. These issues get a lot of press. These issues also generate a lot of donations to politicians on both sides of the debate.

Democracy is a transactional business. In politics, you rarely get everything that you want. To civilly resolve this issue there needs to be some kind of compromise. The idea of making abortion illegal after the first trimester sounds to me to be reasonable.

I line up with the pro-life group on this issue. But as things stand now, we have legal abortion for the full nine months of the pregnancy. The above compromise would eliminate six of those months. It is not a perfect solution, but it is better than what we have now.

As far as other issues are concerned, our tax laws should en-courage marriage and families. We should continue to give tax breaks to families with children. Proper funding of preschool, of school lunch programs, and public education all add to the stability of the family. We should revisit our public aid laws so they promote rather than discourage marriage. The more married families a society can have, the stronger the society will be.

We should not forget older people in this family discussion. The way that many of our current pension plans are written, if a widow or a widower remarries, they automatically lose the pension benefits that they had accrued under their deceased spouse's plan. The result is that they often lose money if they remarry. As a result, many decide to just live with their new loves, rather than marry them.

This sets a bad example for their children and especially their grandchildren. If Grandma doesn't need to get married, why should I worry about it? Families and marriage are about commitments. A society without strong commitments is not a strong society.

The final topic under families is the gay issue. During the Obama administration, laws were written that gave gay partnerships the same status as a marriage between a man and a woman. I do not believe that a gay relationship is the same as a marriage, no matter how kind and loving the relationship may be. Two women can't take the place of a father. And conversely, two men cannot take the place of a mother.

Civil unions should be recognized by law. This legally protects both partners. But this is not the same as a marriage between a man and a woman for the purpose of procreating children. We should not confuse the two.

Chapter Eight

FINAL THOUGHTS

LISTED BELOW ARE a few random thoughts that I picked up along the way.

America was founded on the audacious idea that a country could be ruled by common men just as well as by a king, or by a ruling class. The theory is that many minds were better than one or a few. It was predicated on the notion that reason could control passion. The drama of that idea has played out throughout all of the country's history.

America was fortunate in having very well-educated men involved in its founding. They were well read and well versed in the various forms of government. But even more than that, they were keen observers of the nature of their fellow man. They understood the vagaries of human nature. Men tend to be inconsistent, often change their minds, and don't always act from the highest of motives. Sometimes they are driven by pride and greed, and not by justice and kindness. So, the framers of the Constitution developed a government with checks and balances. They hoped in this way to keep any one branch of government from dominating the others. This checks-and-balances system has worked for over two hundred years.

This unique American experiment offered three things that the people of Europe desired, one was freedom, one was opportunity, and the other was excitement.

In America you had freedom. You could say what you wanted to say without fear of any recrimination. You could worship as you wished, and you could be anything that you were willing to work for. These ideas appealed to Europe's poor and downtrodden.

America also offered excitement. Everything was new. To the new settlers from Europe, the country was a clean slate to be written upon. New things were happening daily before their eyes. It was fun and exciting to get up each morning to see what the day would bring. Life was an adventure.

The new immigrants bought into the vision of what this country could be, and they bought into the American dream. The original dream was adequate shelter, decent clothes to wear, enough food to eat, and sufficient wages to support a family and to educate the children. The American Dream of prior generations has been achieved today by the majority of our citizens. Our housing is adequate. Normally we have enough clothing to wear and food to eat. There is access to higher education. And for the most part, transportation is not a problem. While the American dream has brought comfort, it has not brought us happiness. We want more. But we don't know more of what? The old American Dream catapulted America for the last two centuries. Now we need a new dream to move us for the next two hundred years.

The current American dream is incomplete. It is too self-centered. Or to be blunt about it, it is too selfish. We must realize that we are not the center of the universe. We must realize that there is more to life than fulfilling our own desires. As Americans, we must realize that we make up only 4% of the population of this planet. The new dream must realize that there is another big world beyond our borders. And we must realize that our planet is such a small part of our galaxy. And that beyond the Milky Way galaxy there are millions and millions of more galaxies. Our new dream must contain a sense of proportion. We must realize our small place in creation. We are not masters of our world. At most, we are explorers of it.

The exploration of America created great excitement. Perhaps it is time for Americans to become explorers again. Perhaps it is time to become earnest explorers of our solar system and then of our galaxy. Perhaps it is time to rekindle the excitement again.

Currently, there is an ancestry craze going on in the country. People keep asking the question, who am I? They try to trace their ancestors through public records, family oral history, and now through genetic testing. This is all very interesting. But it is not the question that they should be asking. They should be asking what are we. What does it mean to be a human being in the 21st century? What are our characteristics? What are our strengths and weaknesses? If these questions are asked, they will inevitably come to the conclusion that we are not perfect. We become easily unfocused and sometimes misguided. Realizing that we are not perfect would go a long way to help us work with our fellow man. And we do need to work together. There are a lot of improvements needed in our current world. Remember if you only have perfect people for friends, then you shall not have many friends.

Democracy is a most difficult form of government to direct. Either we are led by our basic instincts—greed, self-interest, power, or pride—or we are led by our highest ideals: justice, courage, and honor and dedication. We face a constant struggle to be led by the higher angels of our nature.

Democracy has sometimes been described as trying to do the impossible with the improbable. Perfection in any endeavor, and especially in a democratic government, is impossible. Humans by our very nature are imperfect creatures. We try but never seem to get things right all the time.

Democracy is based on the assumption that if citizens are presented with all of the facts on an issue, they will come to a reasonable conclusion and course of action. But citizens at the time of the founding of the country were defined as men of property. The Founding Fathers in their wildest imagination never thought that a vagabond or a migrant worker would have the same voice in the national affairs, as that of a landowner. They believed that citizens needed to have a stake in the country, in order to have a voice in it. This would all change in the future with the introduction of universal male suffrage, the Fourteenth Amendment, and later by woman's suffrage. This enlargement of the electorate was to have major repercussions into our modern elections. The universal suffrage we now have is much different from the restricted suffrage as viewed by the writers of the Constitution.

Today's democratic form of government is a rough-and-tumble process. By its nature, it plays to the popular appeal of the electorate. If you step into the arena, you should expect a lot of criticism. There will always be someone who believes that they can do a better job than you.

Democracy by its very nature is a transactional business. It is a constant trading of wants. I will allow you to have something you want, in return for you allowing me to have something that I desire. In this type of environment, no one ever gets all they want. The perfect is usually sacrificed for the better.

I think modern American politics has become more about winning than governing. It has become more about power, prestige, and money. This is to the detriment of both political parties. Most Americans want a government which is fiscally sound, provides the basic services, and protects society. The average American is more interested in his family, his job, his community, and the local sports team than he is about major political issues. As life becomes more hectic and the pace increases, people do not want to spend a lot of time on political issues. They just want the government to work. And they want to be able to get on with their lives.

We need a new kind of gentility born not of weakness or affectation, but of a strong respect for our fellow Americans. We need a strong dose of manners and respect for each other. Once upon a time, the South was famous for this type of etiquette. Wouldn't it be refreshing if that could be reborn?

Everyone is constantly talking about freedom. But freedom needs boundaries and rules in order to be free. Otherwise, we have chaos and anarchy.

We must take responsibility for our actions, and understand that actions have consequences.

Americans have a tendency to think that individual character flaws can be corrected by laws. Experience teaches that this is wrong. Remember the Volstead Act and the Prohibition era? Morality can't be legislated.

The error of the 20th century was not accepting the world as it is but trying to create a new world order. First, it was the idea of a master race and Nazism, and then it was the idea of the equality of all men and Communism. Neither provided the answers. We have to take the world as it is and try to make it better. Creating a world is not our job. God has already done that for us.

We are witnessing the decline of Western Civilization. The Judeo-Christian concept of life has been shaken to its foundation. It seems to be replaced not by any concept of what life means. Its replacement appears to be undirected activity and a blur of information and technology. This is overwhelming individuals. There is no time to think. There is no space in our lives to concentrate on values.

The old guideposts of our culture are fading. Churches, neighborhoods, and family, still resonate with people, but they don't have the attraction that they once held. We have come to a cross road. Do we wish to rekindle the old values which these institutions stood for, or do we wish to plunge forward instituting new values as we try to find our way? The decision is ours to make. Hopefully we will make the correct choice

The two highest callings men can aspire to are serving God and serving each other. If you decide to serve your fellow man, consider spending some time in politics. In normal times the role of a politician would be considered a noble calling. The ancient Greeks and Romans admired their leaders. The founding men of our Republic were held in high esteem. Today things have changed. Politicians are rarely admired. Few parents want their son or daughter to grow up to be a politician. We need men and women of high moral character and integrity to restore the role of a politician to its proper place of honor in our society.

Remember, a good politician tries to serve their fellow citizens. He or she attempts to improve any situation in which their office places them. A good politician should always try to be humble. They are there to serve, not to increase their self-esteem. If you do your job well, you will be held in high regard.

People naturally look up to their elected officials. Try to set a good example by good stewardship and an upright character.

A good politician can't make the community perfect. But they should always make it better.

Your involvement in politics can take many forms; it can be at the local level, the state level, or the national level. Currently, America desperately needs politicians of high character and reputation to take their place in all levels of public office. Personally, I think that it is more difficult to be the mayor of a small town than it is to be president. As president, you have access to many experts and whatever resources that you may need. As mayor of a small town, you are on your own. There is no one protecting you from a screaming citizen on your front porch. Don't consider any office to be too demeaning. The local school board or town council is just as important as Congress or the state legislature.

Both major parties should be promoting individuals of high intelligence and good morals for public office. And those who are elected should conduct themselves so as to be good examples for all those who follow them. Remember that public service is a privilege and not an entitlement. Do not enter politics as a means to obtain wealth.

One of my favorite political stories is about President Harry Truman.

The story is told that a few weeks before his term as president ended, he had to approach a bank for a loan. It seems that Harry did not have enough funds to travel back to his hometown of Independence, Missouri! Here was someone who did not think that public service was to be used as a ticket for wealth.

If you do decide to enter the public arena, realize that politics is a rough-and-tumble business; it attracts people of all persuasion. You will meet men and women of high ideals and morals, and you will meet people who are driven by greed and power. Be alert. Unfortunately, no one wears a name tag.

Have your financing in place before you begin a campaign. Don't think that your good ideas are going to attract sufficient financing. Perhaps they will. But do not depend on it.

And if you should get elected, be humble. Be a good leader. A good leader is someone who galvanizes support for a project. He energizes all who participate in the effort in such a way that when the goal is achieved, the group thinks that the project was their idea and that they did it themselves. This builds a stronger and more self-confident organization. A good leader never makes things about himself. It is always about achieving the objective.

Without economic power, political power is impossible. You must pay attention to the economics of the situation.

So, my grandchildren, there you have it: the reasons that I ran, and some thoughts I picked up along the way.

My campaign was by all measures a complete failure. The fault was all my own. Whatever votes I received in Iowa were placed into the miscellaneous column. In Missouri, I received just a handful of votes. To an outsider, I must have looked like Don Quixote come back to life. I was an old man roving the Midwestern country roads chasing windmills.

For myself, I found the whole experience exhilarating! I met many people of great kindness, goodwill, and decency—people who deserve a competent form of government. This gives me hope for the future. Good luck to those who will take up the challenge and calling of going into politics.

I have no regrets. I will probably never know what effect this effort had, if any. We never know the shadows that we cast. But a person must stand for what they believe. That is what nourishes the soul.

At the end of the day, each of us has to look ourselves in the mirror and hopefully say that we did our best.

You need not be perfect. Just try to do your best.

Good luck with whatever your life's work might be.

Remember, life is an adventure. Don't be afraid. Go out and live the adventure.

Frankfort, Illinois, June 2018

Acknowledgements

I wish to acknowledge those individuals who helped me on this improbable journey.

Pete and Judy Connolly

Bobbie Hayes

Rosemary Homer

Beth McDonough

P.C.Smith

Bill Stouffer

Thank you all very much.